EXPLORING COUNTRIES

Iceland

by Lisa Owings

BLASTOFF!
READERS
5

BELLWETHER MEDIA • MINNEAPOLIS, MN

Note to Librarians, Teachers, and Parents:

Blastoff! Readers are carefully developed by literacy experts and combine standards-based content with developmentally appropriate text.

Level 1 provides the most support through repetition of high-frequency words, light text, predictable sentence patterns, and strong visual support.

Level 2 offers early readers a bit more challenge through varied simple sentences, increased text load, and less repetition of high-frequency words.

Level 3 advances early-fluent readers toward fluency through increased text and concept load, less reliance on visuals, longer sentences, and more literary language.

Level 4 builds reading stamina by providing more text per page, increased use of punctuation, greater variation in sentence patterns, and increasingly challenging vocabulary.

Level 5 encourages children to move from "learning to read" to "reading to learn" by providing even more text, varied writing styles, and less familiar topics.

Whichever book is right for your reader, Blastoff! Readers are the perfect books to build confidence and encourage a love of reading that will last a lifetime!

This edition first published in 2013 by Bellwether Media, Inc.

No part of this publication may be reproduced in whole or in part without written permission of the publisher. For information regarding permission, write to Bellwether Media, Inc., Attention: Permissions Department, 5357 Penn Avenue South, Minneapolis, MN 55419.

Owings, Lisa.
Iceland / by Lisa Owings.
       p. cm. – (Blastoff! readers : exploring countries)
Includes bibliographical references and index.
Summary: "Developed by literacy experts for students in grades three through seven, this book introduces young readers to the geography and culture of Iceland"–Provided by publisher.
ISBN 978-1-60014-762-3 (hardcover : alk. paper)
1. Iceland–Juvenile literature. I. Title.
DL305.O95 2013
949.12–dc23   2012000962

Printed in the United States of America, North Mankato, MN.

Contents

Where Is Iceland?

Did you know?

The northernmost points of Iceland nearly touch the Arctic Circle. This means the sun hardly dips below the horizon in June. In December, the sun is only up for a few hours each day.

Denmark Strait
Greenland Sea
Iceland
Reykjavík
N
W
E
S
Atlantic Ocean

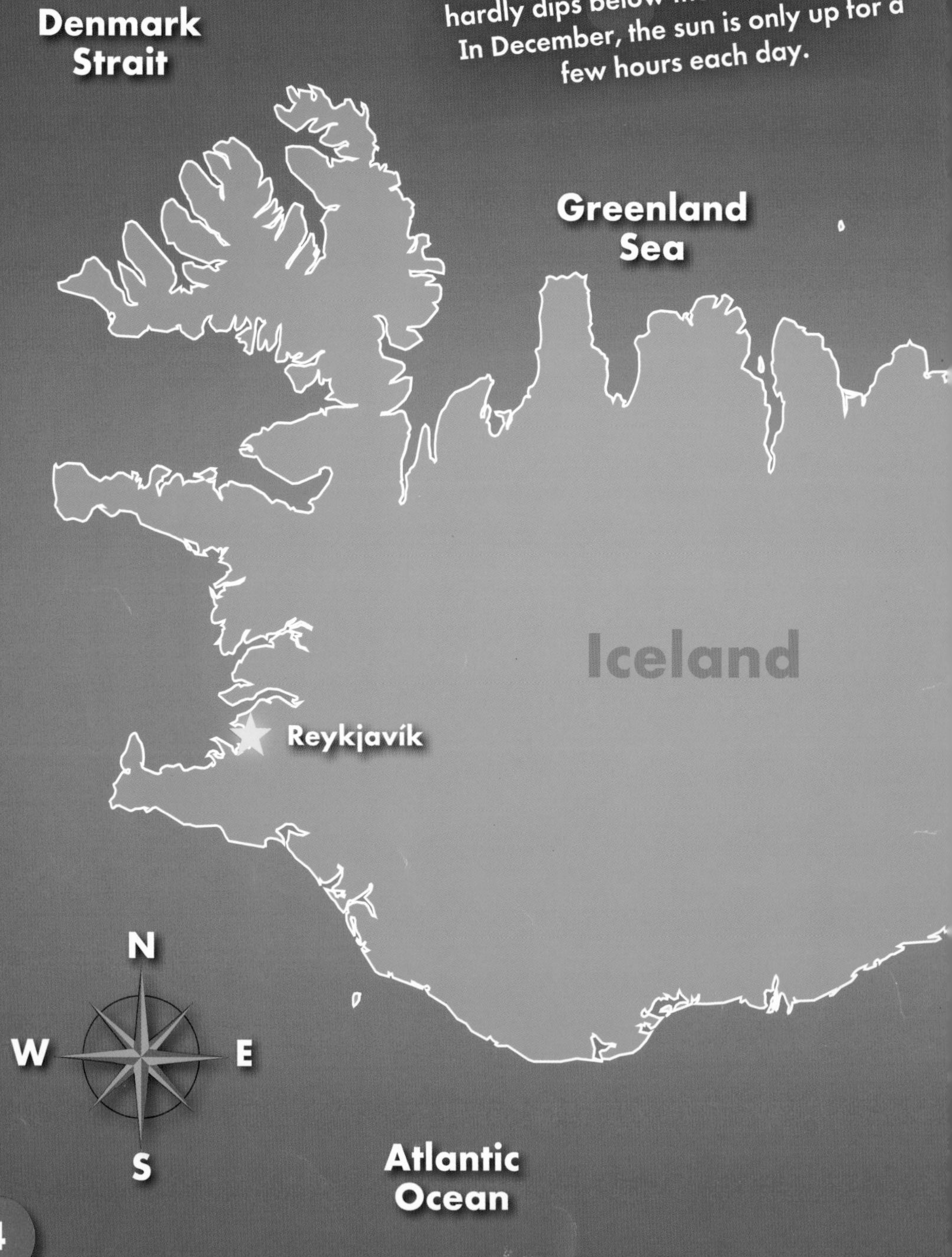

Iceland is a rugged island of tall mountains and deep **fjords**. A part of Europe, the country sits in the chilly Atlantic Ocean. The Greenland Sea touches its northern shores. Across the Denmark **Strait** to the northwest is Iceland's nearest neighbor, Greenland. To the east lies Norway, and the United Kingdom is a short flight to the southeast.

Spanning 39,769 square miles (103,000 square kilometers), Iceland is a small country. Its capital and largest city is Reykjavík. This is the northernmost capital city in the world.

Did you know?

In the spring of 2010, Iceland's Eyjafjallajökull spewed lava and ash into the sky. The eruption made air travel so dangerous that many European airports had to be shut down.

Eyjafjallajökull

In some places, Iceland lives up to its name. **Glaciers** top large areas of the rocky landscape. **Arctic** winds howl through the dark, snowy winters. However, Iceland is also a land of fire. The island rests atop the **Mid-Atlantic Ridge**. This makes Iceland a hot spot for **volcanic eruptions** and mild earthquakes.

fun fact

Iceland has the largest number of hot springs in the world. Some hot springs shoot water into the air. They are called geysers after the Icelandic word *geysir*.

Iceland's landscape is green in the summer, but it has few trees. Clear lakes, sparkling waterfalls, and jagged fjords add to its beauty. The climate does not change much throughout the year. Winters are mild and summers are cool. The average temperature in the capital city is 40 degrees Fahrenheit (4 degrees Celsius).

Vatnajökull

Iceland's Vatnajökull is the largest **ice cap** in Europe. It covers about 3,200 square miles (8,400 square kilometers) of southeastern Iceland. This famous glacier sits atop the country's highest peak, Hvannadalshnúkur. It also stretches over several active volcanoes. Sometimes one of the volcanoes erupts and melts the ice around it. This can cause major floods.

People come from all over the world to see and hike on Vatnajökull. The blue ice and clear lakes make it worth the trip. The largest glacial lake, called Jökulsárlón, is filled with brilliant blue **icebergs** from Vatnajökull.

Jökulsárlón

Arctic fox

gyrfalcon

puffin

Most of Iceland's wildlife arrived by sea or sky. The large white-tailed eagle and the fierce gyrfalcon patrol the skies in search of prey. Ducks, pink-footed geese, and whooper swans bob in cold lakes. Sad-eyed puffins make their homes on cliffs and smaller islands off the coast.

humpback whale

Did you know?

About 20 species of whales have been spotted from Iceland's shores. Whale watchers visit the country to see humpback whales, sperm whales, fin whales, and more.

Offshore, large schools of fish share the sea with lobsters and shrimp. Seals and whales visit Iceland's coasts to feed and raise their young. The only land mammal **native** to Iceland is the Arctic fox. However, people have brought horses, reindeer, and mink to the island. Even polar bears sometimes swim over from Greenland!

Did you know?

The Icelandic Naming Committee must approve every name that has not been used before. The committee decides whether the name reflects Icelandic culture.

More than 300,000 people call Iceland home. Almost all Icelanders have **ancestors** from Norway, Ireland, or Scotland. Only about 1 out of every 20 Icelanders is an **immigrant** from another European country, North America, or Asia.

The country's small size tends to bring Icelanders together. They bond by sharing the **traditions** and beliefs of their ancestors. They also share the Icelandic language, which is very similar to the language of their ancestors.

Speak Icelandic!

English	Icelandic	How to say it
hello	halló	HAH-loh
good-bye	bless	bless
yes	já	yow
no	nei	nay
please	takk	tahk
thank you	takk	tahk
friend	vinur	VEEN-uhr

fun fact

Over half of all Icelanders live in and around Reykjavík.

Though Icelanders remember their roots, they also lead modern lives. More than nine out of every ten Icelanders live in cities near the coast. Icelanders are hard workers, and many hold more than one job. Older children often take summer jobs. Most people earn a good income, but they spend a lot of money on **imported** items.

Icelanders travel by car, bus, or bike, often on bumpy gravel roads. Small airplanes are also a common form of transportation. People return to cozy homes heated by **geothermal** energy. Traditional Icelandic homes were built of **turf** and stone. Today most are made of concrete that can withstand earthquakes.

Where People Live in Iceland

countryside 7%

cities 93%

Did you know?
The northern lights are a common sight on cold Icelandic nights. These ribbons of light can only be seen near the North Pole.

Icelandic children start school around age 6, often after a few years of preschool. All Icelanders are required to attend school until they are 16. They study Icelandic, math, social studies, science, art, and other subjects. Students often begin learning English and Danish before the fifth grade.

After grade ten, most Icelandic students go on to four years of high school. Others attend schools that train them for specific jobs in farming, construction, and other careers. Those who graduate from high school can attend the University of Iceland in Reykjavík or one of several other universities in the country.

Did you know?

Students in Iceland must know how to swim in order to graduate from elementary school.

fun fact

Icelandic farmers use geothermal greenhouses to grow tomatoes, cucumbers, bananas, and other crops. These buildings take heat from the earth to keep plants warm.

Where People Work in Iceland

manufacturing 22%

services 73%

farming 5%

Fishing is Iceland's most important **industry**. Fishers cast their nets into the sea for cod, capelin, and herring. They send their catches to factories where other workers prepare them to be shipped around the world. Farmers raise sheep, chickens, and cows for fresh meat and dairy foods. Iceland has little **fertile** land. Farmers can grow potatoes, hay, and a few other **hardy** crops.

In cities, factory workers produce food products and aluminum. Nearly three out of every four Icelanders have **service jobs** in stores, hospitals, or offices. Tourism is another important industry. Every year, many people come to experience Iceland's rugged beauty.

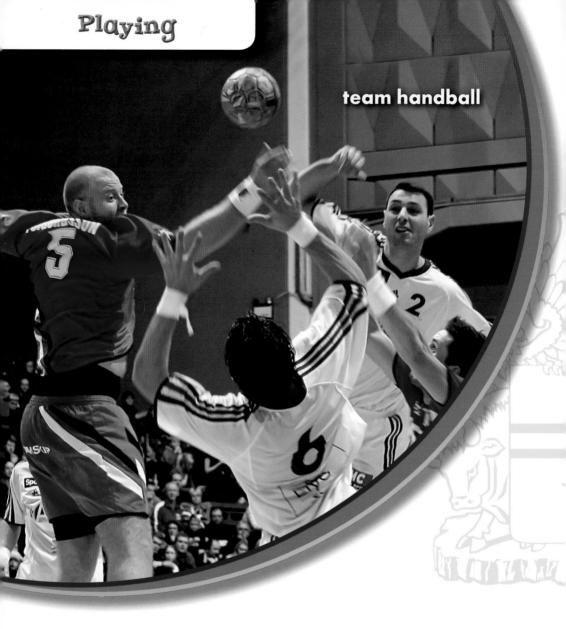

team handball

Icelanders work hard, but they also play hard. Most Icelanders enjoy outdoor activities such as swimming, skiing, horseback riding, and kayaking. After a day of adventuring, a dip in a hot spring is a common way to relax. Popular sports include soccer, **team handball**, and a traditional form of wrestling called *glíma*.

City-dwelling Icelanders love to go out to movies and concerts. They get especially excited to see Icelandic musicians such as Björk and Sigur Rós. On quieter evenings, people challenge one another to games of chess, curl up with a book, or do some traditional knitting.

Did you know?
Iceland is one of the best places in the world for ice climbing. Daring women and men use ropes and axes to help them climb up frozen waterfalls!

Did you know?

Hot dog stands are popular throughout Iceland. Instead of pork, the hot dogs are made of lamb. Icelanders top them with ketchup, mustard, and onions.

Meat dominates the typical Icelandic diet. Fish and lamb are **staples**. *Gravlax* is a popular dish of salmon seasoned with salt and dill. Market stalls offer *harðfiskur*, a snack of dried fish served with butter. *Svið* has been made in Iceland for over 1,000 years. This dish is made by cutting a sheep's head in half and boiling it. *Hangikjöt*, or smoked lamb, is often part of holiday feasts.

Icelanders sip coffee or tea with a light breakfast of toast or cereal. Soup and rye bread make a warm, simple lunch. Dinner is the main meal in Iceland. Meat or fish is often served with potatoes. Icelanders enjoy *skyr* for dessert. Similar to yogurt, it is often topped with fruit.

fun fact

A traditional midwinter dish called *hákarl* is prepared by cutting up shark meat and letting it rot for a few months.

hákarl

skyr

Arts Festival

Christmas Yule Lads

Icelanders love a good party. Each New Year begins with bonfires, feasts, and fireworks. The *Þorrablót* Festival stretches from January into February. This winter feast features many of Iceland's traditional foods. With spring come Easter egg hunts and more feasts. The Arts Festival in May draws many citizens and tourists to Reykjavík.

Sjómannadagurinn is a June festival that celebrates the sea. Many Icelanders compete in swimming and rowing events. Parades and speeches mark Independence Day on June 17. Icelanders in the east greet winter by telling ghost stories and going for nighttime walks during the Days of Darkness Festival. Christmas celebrations involve 13 days of feasting and gift-giving.

Many Icelanders believe they share their island with elves, trolls, and other **mythical** beings. These beings are linked to Iceland's history and landscape. Elves are called *huldufólk*, or "hidden people." They are thought to live in rocks and make mischief if their homes are disturbed.

Trolls are ugly and not very nice. However, they always keep their promises. Trolls turn to stone if sunlight touches them. Many rock formations in Iceland are said to be trolls. The magic of Icelandic **folklore** brings Icelanders together, and its stories and traditions help them remember their past.

elf home

Hvítserkur

Fast Facts About Iceland

Iceland's Flag

The Icelandic flag features a red cross with a white border on a blue background. The cross is a symbol of Iceland's Scandinavian heritage. The blue represents the sea and sky. The white represents snow and ice. Red stands for fire. It is also the color of Denmark, the country from which Iceland gained independence in 1944.

Official Name: Republic of Iceland

Area: 39,769 square miles (103,000 square kilometers); Iceland is the 108th largest country in the world.

Capital City:	Reykjavík
Important Cities:	Kópavogur, Hafnarfjörður, Akureyri
Population:	311,183 (July 2012)
Official Language:	Icelandic
National Holiday:	Independence Day (June 17)
Religions:	Christian (87.2%), Other (9.8%), None (3%)
Major Industries:	energy, fishing, manufacturing, services, tourism
Natural Resources:	fish, hydropower, geothermal energy
Manufactured Products:	aluminum, fishing equipment, cement, food products, clothing, books
Farm Products:	sheep, chicken, beef, dairy products, wool, potatoes
Unit of Money:	Icelandic króna; the króna is divided into 100 aurar.

Glossary

ancestors—relatives who lived long ago

arctic—relating to the northern part of the world

fertile—able to support growth

fjords—long, narrow inlets of the ocean between tall cliffs; fjords are formed by the movement of glaciers.

folklore—stories, customs, and beliefs that are handed down from one generation to the next

geothermal—using heat from deep within the earth

glaciers—massive, slow-moving sheets of ice

hardy—strong, healthy, and able to survive in harsh conditions

ice cap—a permanent covering of ice and snow

icebergs—large pieces of ice that have broken off glaciers and are floating in water

immigrant—a person who leaves one country to live in another country

imported—brought into the country from somewhere else

industry—a branch of business or production in a country; farming, fishing, and services are kinds of industries.

Mid-Atlantic Ridge—the meeting point of two main sections of Earth's crust; the gradual movement of these sections causes earthquakes and volcanoes.

mythical—imaginary or based on old stories and beliefs

native—originally from a specific place

service jobs—jobs that perform tasks for people or businesses

staples—products that are widely and regularly used

strait—a narrow stretch of water that connects two larger bodies of water

team handball—a sport similar to soccer in which the ball is thrown instead of kicked to make a goal

traditions—stories, beliefs, or ways of life that families or groups hand down from one generation to the next

turf—grass and the top layer of earth beneath it

volcanic eruptions—explosions of lava, steam, and ash; over time, volcanic eruptions can form mountains.

To Learn More

AT THE LIBRARY

Fradin, Judith Bloom. *Volcano! The Icelandic Eruption of 2010 and Other Hot, Smoky, Fierce, and Fiery Mountains.* Washington, D.C.: National Geographic, 2010.

Kane, Doug, and Christy Wood. *Ariel's Journey.* Amherst, Ohio: Blue Ink Press, 2008.

Miller, Jennifer A. *Iceland.* Minneapolis, Minn.: Lerner Publications, 2011.

ON THE WEB

Learning more about Iceland is as easy as 1, 2, 3.

1. Go to www.factsurfer.com.

2. Enter "Iceland" into the search box.

3. Click the "Surf" button and you will see a list of related Web sites.

With factsurfer.com, finding more information is just a click away.

Index